THE HABIT OF HOPE

THE HABIT OF HOPE

Poems by

Dawn E. Morrow

Antrim House
Bloomfield, Connecticut

Library of Congress Control Number: 2022919655

ISBN: 979-8-9865522-0-0

First Edition

Printed & bound by Ingram Content Group

Book design by Rennie McQuilkin

Cover painting by Holly Carton

Author photograph by Sarah Breck

Antrim House
860.217.0023
AntrimHouseBooks@gmail.com
www.AntrimHouseBooks.com
400 Seabury Dr., #5196, Bloomfield, CT 06002

For my mom, who was the first to call me a writer

ACKNOWLEDGMENTS

Thanks to the editors of the following publications, in which poems from this volume first appeared, sometimes in earlier versions:
The Molehill: "The Garden State" and "On Having Upstairs Neighbors"
The Rabbit Room blog: "Notre Dame in Flames"
SLAB: "Elegy for the Unknown," "Lionheart," and "Smoke"

Deepest thanks to my family: Ru, Kim, Lily, and Jacob Sen; Eric, Liz, Zeke, and Eli Larson, Lisa and Lily Easterbrooks; Dan, Lynda, Emily, Ben, Joey, and Lucy Adamson; Jon, Kristin, Maggie, Bekah, Abby, Kyle, and Ben Nelson; Anthony, Michelle, Isaiah, and Israel Johnson; and Ryan and Charissa Shelton. You have kept me fed and sane through years of writing, and all the years before that. I wouldn't be who I am without you. I love you.

Thanks to Jenn DeSalle, my oldest friend and partner in crime, who appears unnamed in more than one of these poems.

Thank you to Dax Hock, Ami Rich, and Doug Silton. These poems had been around for a while, but this book was truly born in Portugal. Thanks for adventuring with me. Let's do it again.

Unending gratitude to my writing partners Megan Murai, Jane Scharl, Julie Sumner, CJ Surbaugh, and Hallie Waugh. You were my first readers, my last readers, and all the readers in between. Thank you for your encouragement, partnership, and commiseration.

Jeanne Murray Walker and Bob Cording, thank you for being the best mentors I could have asked for. You pushed me outside my comfort zone, challenged me to be better and offered gracious criticism. Thank you for believing in my poems. Colleen Cording, thank you for opening your life up to all of us. I am a better person for it.

Thank you to Luci Shaw for your incisive critique. Because of you I grew into more than a one-trick pony.

Jonathan Rogers, without you I would not have found my voice, and I am forever grateful.

Finally, thanks to Antrim House and Rennie McQuilkin for making this book come to life. Thank you for your faith in my work and your edits to my poems. I am proud of what we've made together.

TABLE OF CONTENTS

This is the year when laughter douses charred and burnt-out dreams.
This is the year when wrens return to nest in storm-blown trees.
Is this the year of relocation from boughs of old despair?
This is the year to perch on hope's repair.

"New Year" Eric Peters

THE HABIT OF HOPE

Sounds Like Lace

When Luci wrote of the ebbtide
sounds like lace, I returned
to early mornings, shore front,
bare feet on wet sand,
my uncles on the pier casting lines
or pulling up crab traps full
of clicking claws we'd throw
in a pot of boiling water
'til they came to the color
of the sun on the bay side
of the island. This year
seems like the tide has gone
out so far it's uncovered
all the lost things swept
to sea: seaweed tangled
in rusted gears; a mangled
mess of crushed-up shell,
remains of seagull snacks;
and here and there, the bright
blue glint of sea glass,
edges worn smooth, frosted
by years of tides, the water
swaying like a woman
who dances to the memory
of a song she used to know.

Nowhere, Really

When people ask, "Where are you from?"
I answer "Nowhere, really." But I walk two blocks
to the fishpond, only recalled
by a perfect circle of freshly mown grass
behind the old tabernacle whose bells still peal
at a pitch that resonates deep in my chest.

In the bag of frozen bread swinging from my wrist,
I feel the rhythm of a hundred summer Saturdays
and relish the liturgies of my childhood,
my grandmother, its cantor.
I kneel, and press my hands to the ground
as if the earth itself shares my history;
as if it would awaken and remind me of all the things
I have forgotten, my memories like the yellowed lace
under the candy dish on my grandma's coffee table.

Down at the surf, they are dredging,
long steel pipes spraying clouds
of deep-sea sand back onto the beach it came from.

Remembering My Father on Father's Day

My Father exists in flashes of memory
I may have cobbled together from boxes
of pictures I collected from my mother's house
after she died. In one, we lie on the old brown couch
they imported from the Seventies. He tosses
a brown crocheted pillow at the mutt named
after the booze nobody liked, hidden
in the back of the liquor cabinet.
The dog is in midair, her body twisted
to catch it like a stuffed frisbee. We are laughing
and somewhere, behind the camera,
my mother scolds, but she laughs too.
And that is why I think this memory
might be real: that laughter, hanging
there like a phantom limb.

Earworm

I can't say for sure how I know the song played
by the ghostly pianist at the grocery store,
but I sing, *the girl from Ipanema goes walking* –
the only lyrics I know. It must have been
a remnant of my mother who sang scraps
of songs to whoever happened to cross her path,
waltzing through the kitchen crooning *Getting to know you*
to her brand new nephew, or humming
I feel pretty to my grandmother's cat
as she worked the tangles out of its long orange hair.
In the store, the piano stops playing,
but her essence lingers like confetti
caught in the cushion of the couch
years after the party ended.

Hands-On

I wish I'd paid closer attention
to my grandmother as she shaped
yarn into the afghan that covers
my legs. My fingers itch to create
something tangible, to coax plants
from fresh-tilled soil or a bowl
from a lump of clay. But my garden
is a cemetery of cucumber vines,
and I never learned to knit or sculpt,
so my hands lie fallow, waiting
for words, wishing they had
a mind of their own.

Visiting Hours

Pipe smoke and sawdust, the essence of my grandfather,
grey felt fedora tipped a little to the left. He puttered
around his basement shop and I built towers
from the blocks he'd cut on the table saw.
He held my hands in his and guided wood
across blade to create triangles and squares,
the table's vibration moving up my arms and into the core
of my body, resonating like a cleanly struck tuning fork.
After my father left, my mom found two hand-pieced
lamps in our foyer, stacked wood slices twisted together
into a braid. The note said, *Love, George*. I understood:
You're still family. I'm still here.
When I learned to drive, I visited him, an hour away,
navigating with paper map and memory, driving down one road
then another until I found the house. Tongue and hands
stroke-slowed, he'd given up the saw years before,
so we sat together in the company of the football commentator
and just before I left, I told him: "I'm still here."

Aviator

Dad tinkered with radios
that never worked,
the smell of hot solder mingling
with the oil-and-cigarette-smoke
cologne that clung to him.

I played in the pilot's seat
of the wingless airplane
in our garage, waving hello
to the poster of the pink-feathered
dancing girl as I flew past.

My grandfather was a pilot.
My mother was a stewardess.
My father flew on fantasies.
I was fearless.
I didn't know planes could crash.

I flew over the house
and saw it recede into
a child's drawing – all
triangles and squares.
I flew around the world

I knew only through
Disney World and landed
in the kitchen where my mom
set the table for dinner.
She'd forgotten how to fly.

When she told me to get my father
I flew from kitchen to garage,
bare feet slapping on slate floor,
arms outstretched. With my wings
I covered the miles in between them.

From the Scrapbook

My mother, young, blue-suited,
carrying white roses, hand-in-hand
with my father whose mouth
is open, cracking a joke. She smiles
at the camera – not at the joke.
These people, before. Before life
settles down around their shoulders,
puts them in 9-5 jobs. Before cancer
claims one grandmother and a stroke
another. Everyone is happy here –
or fakes it well; hope floats
like a buoy to flag the moment.
Remember, remember this later
when it all goes to shit:
Once upon a time you were happy.

Reseeding Memory

The jacket in my closet still smells
like smoke and oil, like just cut grass.
My father mowed; I played outside. He teased
circles around the swing set as I dangled
from the crossbar, kicking tickling fingers
away from bare feet. No trace
of ever-present beer cans, just the sun
casting long shadows over his face
as he surveyed his work: even, green,
neat rows where he'd taught me to throw
softballs and horseshoes. Finished, he turned
and his eyes gathered the scene: my tan body
outgrowing the little girl chair I sat in.
He held his hand to mine, comparing
the size, then swung me up onto his shoulders.
I could see everything. It was his last summer there.

Shrunk

My father came home most nights,
stripped off work clothes, and pulled
at mud-splattered boots, the soles stuck
with fiberglass shards;
and after a quick, quiet dinner,
fell asleep in his chair: feet up,
TV on, Budweiser cans on the end table.
His snores, my lullaby.

But some nights, he rubbed his hands
over his favorite white thermal shirt, jumping sparks
orange magic in the dimness, delighted
by my laughter. One winter, after
he'd been gone three nights, my mother ran
the dryer hot, until my doll could wear
the shirt, the magic all washed out.
He never came home to bring it back.

The Moonflowers

When summer sun dropped low enough
to cast our shadows long and lean,
we gathered in the neighbor's yard,
waiting for the moonflowers to bloom.

Pavement hot against bare feet, we jumped
from sidewalk on to grass, cooling our soles,
rough from days of running free. Our parents
drank from plastic cups of boxed red wine or Bud.

Summer by summer, our number dwindled,
divorce and aging taking their toll.

Still, every evening we watched
until the little flowers quivered,
loosening their buds, and the first flower
shook its petals free.

One by one they popped open
until an entire bouquet of white trumpets
heralded their own arrival, as if announcing
sometimes beauty comes at night.

Busted

After the hurricane we snuck to the corner
flooded with dirty water
and floated my mother's brand new
umbrella in the stream as it rushed by.
Should have gotten away with it –
a longer than usual stroll to the 7-11
at the end of the block, time spent
making crucial decisions about penny candy
or Slurpees. Even the umbrella made it back.
Then, the morning paper, just below the fold
the caption – *Two girls play with umbrella
in flood water*: me, tilted forward,
mom's umbrella in hand, and Jen,
using hers to protect us both
from the end of storm drizzle.
The street signs perfectly positioned
above our heads might as well have said "liars."

Headstrong (Adj) – Very Stubborn

On the two-block walk to work,
my friend adds *headstrong*
to the string of words used
to describe me. It crashes
into *bossy* and *emotional*
and settles there, like the pendant
hanging from the chain
around my neck. *Bullheaded*
was the word my babysitter used
when I refused to yield.
I pictured great horns budding
just above my ears, the kids
around me falling silent,
awed by my emerging strength.

Evolution

I learned to use a revolving door
in the fanciest hotel I'd ever seen.
The first try tossed me out –
back onto the sidewalk
where my mother laughed. She offered
to demonstrate, then seemed surprised
when I wedged myself in next to her
in the pie-shaped space. No room
for two of us, I pressed flat
against the wall, arms splayed
like the wings of a butterfly pinned
to a specimen board. She, on tiptoe,
moved with tiny steps; together
in some strange choreography, counting
time like ballroom dancers,
we emerged, somehow still on our feet.

Garden

Tomatoes grew thick along the back
fence, pulling themselves up
along the wires of their cages, tiny
green fruits appearing, then reddening.
We ate them right off the vines,
sun-warmed flesh, as big as my heart.
In biology we held up our fists
to show the size of the organ
whose beat echoed in my ears at night,
the center of me, strong
and fragile – the way the tomato skin,
once pierced, pours out everything
it has to offer. Even after it's gone,
its smell lingers on my hands, a tribute
to the soil that gave it life: an echo,
a memory, a grief.

Legacy

I creamed together butter and sugar
until it was as yellowy-soft
as the new chicks at the science museum
and remembered how my grandmother
held her hand over both of mine
moving the old green mixer around the bowl.
"Make sure you get it all," she'd say,
"and keep your fingers back."

I leveled out flour in a red cup measure
and imagined Mrs. Smith saying,
"Dry measures are for dry ingredients
and wet measures for wet."
She'd fail you if you got that wrong,
and you'd be on dish duty the next day.

I rolled dough into balls and dropped them
on the sheet, counting – five rows of four –
as Aunt Marie did winter after winter.
And when my mom lost her job,
I slid a spatula under perfectly round cookies,
moving them from baking sheet to cooling rack.
I didn't know what else to do.

Picking Up the Spare

I lived twenty-eight years before anyone I knew
died and then they dropped one after another,
like bowling pins.

At twenty-nine I carried our family stories
alone – great aunt Edna, who made her wayward husband
live in the basement when he showed up again
after so many years, she'd declared
him dead and collected the insurance money.

Or how, when my mother was born,
while my grandfather flew
over Germany, cleaning up
after World War II, his sergeant made sure
he'd been home in the last nine months
before announcing, "It's a girl."

Sometimes I tell our stories to friends
over a glass of wine on the patio, changing a detail
here and there until I'm not sure what's true.
But it doesn't really matter,
because I am the only daughter of the last daughter,

a cliché: the end of the line; the last leaf on the family tree.
And, when I stepped on a hidden sheet of ice,
hands full, and fell, striking my head against
the deck, I thought death
had finally come to finish the frame.

Last Words

I saw my grandmother for the last time
sitting up in bed, worn quilt from
the rehab center tucked around her.
From the other side of the curtain
her roommate's family sang
The First Noel and *Silent Night*.

When silence fell, my grandmother seized
the opportunity. Artificial larynx
turned to maximum volume,
her robotic voice filled the room.
"Too much fucking!" she announced,
holding up her book.

A shirt-free man and buxom woman
entangled on the lurid cover.
The last time I saw my grandmother,
she was hunched over, shoulders shaking,
her wheezy laugh following my mother
as she dragged me out the door.

Perchance to Dream

I don't want to sleep, because when I do
she is there, laughing.
She doesn't know yet.
She hasn't called to say
the doctor found something and it's not good,
hasn't moved into my too-small apartment,
hasn't lost her hair, hasn't heard the chemo pump breathe.
She hasn't met the students who will learn
how a rectal tumor feels by practicing on her.

The Waning Days

She tells me a story, then the same,
ten minutes later like it's not the one
she's told me each time I've visited
this month. When she can't quite follow
the conversation, she smiles, nods,
a visitor in a land where she doesn't speak
the language. She searches for words
as if she didn't spend her entire life
sculpting them into lines and stanzas.
Some days, she is angry –
words snapped out whip-sharp,
but today, she releases them
one or two at a time. I am watching
her fade like the trees on the mountain
spending the last of their power
to explode into color before they shed
their leaves to meet the winter.

Nativity

Mary and Joseph embrace
as if they haven't seen each other in a year,
looking down at the baby they just met,
while in the corner my mother dies, a little
more with every breath.

The radio plays *Silent Night*
for the sixty-fourth time today,
but it can't drown out
the clicking in her throat.

My mother sleeps,
her nose tucked under the crook
of her arm, like a bird resting
after a long day of flying,
beneath the glow of
white lights adorning the tree
we hung our memories on.

Ashes

In winter the beach bleeds all its color out,
and in the midst of the gray: my mother,
on a bench watching the sea.

Her favorite season. Crowds gone,
storefronts boarded, no caramel corn or hot dogs
overpowering the smell of sharp January air.

I watched her watch the waves that day.
Now I wonder if she wrote her instructions then,
considering the way the wind scattered the sand:

Bring me home. The five pounds
of her arrived by mail one winter morning.
We went to the beach one more time,

her fine ash mingling with sand
and sea, all gray. I breathed in salt air, then breathed
her from my palm, like a child blowing kisses.

Ten Years After the Casket Closes

It's not a shadow she left to darken
the days: more like a wisp of the going-out
perfume she dabbed at the base of her throat
where her pulse beat under her fingers.
I handed her bobby pins as she pulled
her long black hair into a bun and secured it
at the nape of her neck just at the place my father
loved to kiss her while she smiled
and I squealed. More like the whisper of prayer
breathed over her dreaming child, carried
in from the back seat after a day
at the beach, hand relaxing just enough
to spill found shells onto the sheets
I've been tucked into.
Or the lively flicker of candles on an 8th birthday cake
before I finally blow them out.

The Boneyard

After the storm
the hinges creaked
on the heavy cellar door
and the rough wood scraped
across the palms of my hands.

The sky was grey
and there was much more
to see now that the trees
were splintered or
blown down.

I sat on the curb,
scraping mud from my shoes,
wondering where
the mail would go
as the neighbors

laid a bright blue tarp
over the pile of
my tangled home
like a quilt over a corpse
before she's taken away.

Ghosts

I dared to sketch you into my future,
lead-grey lines, barely more than shading –
hint of head, hands, torso, feet, hovering
in the background of family vacations
and parties. Cautious discussions of what
we might do next week, next month, next year.
Then you were silent, weekend plans
half-finished, calls unreturned, questions
unanswered, as if you had never existed at all.
I took the nub of my eraser, scratched you
off the ragged page as best I could,
and started the drawing again.

On Day Two

We woke up together
for the first time,
I reached up to feel
my sprayed-stiff hair
crackle under my fingers.

My face felt tight
under all the makeup
I hadn't taken off
when, caught between
delirium and ecstasy,
we tumbled into bed laughing.

When I reached for you,
my hand grasped
a cool sheet.
I heard you before
I rolled over to see you
sitting in that rose-red chair
where my wedding dress had landed
the night before.

White tulle and lace
crumpled under you
filling the space
around your legs.
You held your head
in your hands
and said "I think
we made a mistake."

Our Last Thanksgiving

A motley crew: outcasts and exiles
from all over town with one thing
in common—nowhere else to go.
So we sat, breaking silence
with bland praise
as we reached for the salt.

When the silence stretched
long – too long
even for our awkward host –
he'd pull out his phone
and read a historical fact
about Pilgrims and Indians,
the first Thanksgiving.

I was glad when, after pie and coffee,
the first person excused herself,
leaving us free to follow.
We looked at each other and agreed,
for the first time in months:
Let's never do that again.

Upon Hearing His Name

Images, like the street lit
by lightning, flashing memory
into stop-motion film;
like the dancers at the college raves
in the old church by my dorm,
exposed by the strobe as they danced;
the stage, fingers on ukulele strings,
half eaten burgers, a beer bottle
spun between restless hands,
entire night a chimera of desperation and dread,
like shoots from a dying stump,
struggling to regrow the tree.

Womanhood Lost

At church, on Mother's Day,
we thank the Lord for this,
a woman's highest calling:
to be a mother.

I have never carried a baby,
belly growing, hipbones folding down,
preparing to open like hangar doors
to propel that little body out.

I haven't birthed a baby,
in pain until the doctor
places a red-faced newborn
on my stomach.

Nor lifted a fussy baby
to me, bared my breast
and let her suck nourishment
from my body.

Now my body is a withered vine,
too old to bear fruit.
I'm barely 40, but it's too late.

As if realizing his mistake,
the priest prays for all
those women who are like
mothers – who love other women's children.

The Garden State

Sunday afternoons, in the Garden State,
my father fiddled with the greenhouse
heaters at Mazza's place.

He got paid in seedlings – future tomatoes
and peppers. My mom held them close
to her face, eyes closed, nose to leaves,
breathing in smells of soil and hope.

Sometimes I feel a shadow of guilt buying tomatoes
from the grocery store, picked by strangers
struggling to make a living
by moving from farm to farm.

I should be able to coax red fruit from the soil
and eat tomatoes hot from the vine, as I did once,
a bumper crop: May to November – so many tomatoes
I begged my friends to take them away.

I haven't grown one thing since. The plants,
if they grow at all, are fruitless.
Maybe we have a quota in life – only so much
to yield, and I spent mine all in one place.

Life, Revised

On a small Broadway stage the Titanic sinks
every night and twice on Wednesdays. We watch
the shipbuilder change the plans – correct
design flaws. Hindsight is 20/20,
life working up to the big reveal.
The dripping roof, disregarded, becomes
a trickle, then a flood; or the man you love
leaves your bed, your house, your life.

Who wouldn't want to change the story?
Say no to a second date. Call the contractor
a few days sooner. Build the walls higher
so when the iceberg strikes, the ship floats
just long enough to save everyone. Hindsight –
the spotlight on the things we could have done
before there was nothing left to save.

On Writing First Drafts

Some poems can't be shared
even with the lover who knows
the contours of my body like the hometown
streets he could walk with his eyes closed.
They are barely cooked meat
oozing too-pink juice; the lungs
of a 33-weeker drying out
in the NICU. They are my wild parts
set free to explore the world they try to capture.

On Trying to Write a Love Poem

Before they can be confined to a page
feelings have to mellow. Steep in hot water
until they release their flavor to be held
in the mouth and savored without biting.
New love, for example: not so much a tender
shoot, but a bucking horse, its rider clinging
on until, tired, it yields to the partnership,
both broken into the other, leather loafers
on feet which have forgotten their blisters.

Creation Story

In the beginning, *Hello,* across the void
of the unfamiliar, and it was good.
Or, maybe not, maybe tentative,
maybe forced, maybe two toddlers
throwing sand, a confetti of welcome
that gets in eyes and forces tears,
surprising them both.
Later, *How's it going?* He means it –
or he doesn't: means
I have better things to do or *I have
so many things I want to say,* questions
hidden like kisses in an Easter egg.
And then *See you tomorrow*
or *next week* or *around.* She wonders
if he's saying he hopes he will,
or if he's glad to be walking away –
if he'll walk so far, ever come back again.

In the Subtext

When I say, "You're my favorite
person," I mean I can't imagine
life without you, but I also mean
please don't leave me but if you do,
make it quick – a head-shot, here
and then gone. Not the slow lingering
of a cancer patient desperate
for the next new treatment.
I mean I love you, but I don't know
how this will play out in a year,
or three or ten, so let's not say it.
I worry this like an eight-year-old
with a loose tooth, probe it with my tongue
to see if it's still there, to see if it hurts.

Dehydration

Along the trail, a single purple thistle
stood at attention. Even the cars racing
by on the highway couldn't move it.
I stopped to look, grateful for a reason
to rest. Four miles didn't seem so long
until the clouds scattered and midsummer
sun spread across the path. I wondered
if it had been spared by a merciful mower
and watched its flock be taken down,
or if the flower sprang up, independent,
from an errant seed dropped by a passing bird.
I've walked an hour, and I'm wilting,
my fingers swelling, sweat trickling into my eyes,
regretting my lack of water. But here's
the thistle. It hasn't rained in days
and yet it's undeterred:
the little captain of its spread of grass.

Autumnal Equinox

Praise to the last watermelon
of the season, red flesh pressed
close to green-striped skin.
It cracks under the blade
of my knife, bleeding juice
across the counter, drips
from the edge, leaving pink splatter
across the hem of my yellow t-shirt. Strange,
how little scent the fruit has,
until I find the shirt, days later,
still stained, perfuming my room
with the sharp smell of fermentation,
its sweet juice curved to acid,
as if it mourned the last days of summer.

Terror

Before the radio told me, I only knew
rotation and revolution, the earth on its axis
and then around the sun. But now I know the sun
turns, spins around the Milky Way, which moves
around the universe. Planet, solar system, galaxy,
universe, nesting dolls among billions: the vastness
steals my breath, too big for comprehension.
I'd rather return to a smaller knowing, second
grade understanding of the sun and earth. Simple –
not the complexity of a million moving parts
all making their own path, with no one to steer
the train but habit and hope.

By Any Other Name

I hold the rose at arm's length,
lest I catch its smell, so distinctive
we use it to describe my powder –
rose scented; my bath bomb – rose petal,
which when I drop it in two feet of hot water
smells like my grandmother
just after she spritzed rose water
on her face to unclog her pores.
I tended roses once. They grew
wild and rangy, offering pink and white
bouquets like a new lover. Cut back
every year, they resurrected in the spring.
And when they bloomed, their perfume danced
through the back door of the house
to decorate the kitchen where I cooked
for my husband, their throbbing scent
reminding me of so many gravesides
I nearly lost my breath.

The Stuff of Legends

The smell of the first fires of fall always conjures
my father, burning gypsy moth caterpillars
off the old pear tree before they could eat
every green thing in our backyard.
I'd learned to hate the stinging things
and watched them shrivel under the heat
of the blowtorch, curling into a tight ball
before dropping to the ground with a plop
like the first fat raindrops of a thunderstorm.

On River Road this year, thick white webs
adorn the high tree branches, heralding
the arrival of the gypsy moths again. I tell
my eight-year-old about the smoking husks
of caterpillars, but she is appalled
by the destruction of those butterflies to be.
She doesn't understand the difference.
So I explain: my father was a knight,
defending his land from the evil scourge
which threatened to destroy everything.
I don't tell her the pear tree died anyway.

Notre Dame in Flames

One April the gargoyles awakened,
carved chimera breathing fire, alive
for the first time in nine hundred years.
They rose, wings outstretched, on plumes
of smoke high over the city. For miles
around, people stopped, craning their necks
to see fingers of fire wrap around the cathedral's
spire, and topple it like a child's block tower.

Thousands of miles away, I watch, transfixed
by flame-tails trailing across darkening sky,
the sunset overshadowed by the orange-red
glow of the church as it burned. Not long before,
I stood under the rose window, spellbound,
bell-song resonating deep in my chest,
calling the faithful to prayer.

In Paris, the people press in, held back
by police lines and firemen. They watch
the glow ebb and flow, as if it breathed,
and they sing, as desperate as Orpheus
to bring her back: *Ave Maria, Pray for us.*
They raise the song like a knight's sword
at the dragon's throat.

Sunset

He looked so intently, I turned
and followed his gaze, expecting
something of note, but all I saw
were clouds, blushing
from the evening attention
of the sun. He said, "I forgot
how pretty the sky was." He'd lost
it in the glare of the New York skyline
and I'd lost it in the shadow
of my own apathy.

Concentration

She is picky about her flowers,
not like the moths who live
their whole lives in the few
acres of this garden. The monarch
flits from blossom to blossom;
my presence so near I could run
my finger over her feathery wing
can't distract her from her milkweed search.
It's a freedom: single-minded focus
indifferent to all potential
danger, the same way a toddler
launched himself across the grass
after a group of wrens to see
them take off, not ever noticing
the man on the mower who'd stopped
just shy of him.

Dear Jane, Remember

How the cluster of koi fought for one bite
of shadows flirting with the edges of green
water. Storm clouds passing over bright Santa Fe
sun fooled the orange-tailed fish – they battled
for empty nourishment, solid bodies thrashing
water splashes toward your sandaled toes.
You barely noticed, chin in hand, lost.
I stopped to ask if you were ok; you said, "I am
dwelling in my rich inner life," patting the rock
beside you so I could dwell too. Sometimes,
when city noise below my window startles
me from sleep, I think of you, far away,
breathing *shh* over a restless baby, words
overtaken by exhaustion. Despairing
you may never find your way back.
But see, I bring you a bouquet
of koi, lean over your daughter
and say, "Ah look:
your rich inner life."

Smoke

An hour ago I heard the three-tone chord
of a car wreck nearby: screech, crunch, wail.
Now, parked just across the street,
the car, its driver's side door
bent at an awkward angle, like a broken bone.
The empty udder of the airbag covers the window.
On her balcony, above the remains,
my neighbor grills, smoke seeping from the charcoal,
and when she opens the lid, it surges
upward on the breeze, an offering to the gods,
a celebration of life, of survival, a near miss.

Signs

Hiking down the streets of the city, by pigeons
pecking the sidewalk near a statue
of an old man nobody remembers,
I find no path in a snowy wood, only
remains of someone's lunch and a sign,
discarded – *Please help, I'm hungry.*

Poems still sprout in the city: tentative flowers pressing
through cracked pavement, a monarch flirting
with the hood of my car on the way home,
and tonight, among the ruins
of an abandoned tenement,
a church with its bells ringing.

Echoes

The moon hangs large and low over the lake,
surveying my 'hood, where the bangers
trade dime bags and bullets up the block.
Next door my neighbor is yelling,

her nightly benediction echoing
off our houses' brick fronts as she invites
us to fuck ourselves. She cusses me to sleep.
I dream of driving up a mountain,

climbing a fire tower, and watching the sun set.
When the stars come out, he slips
a ring on my finger; we toast the moon.
The dream slips into nightmare.

When I wake up, the yelling has stopped
and the mountain is a dim memory, like the echo of a scream.

Lionheart

Black cat sleeps, peaceful, at my feet
as if she's always known this life,
but a torn ear and the scar above her eye
betray her story: she came from the streets.
This warm Chicago afternoon persuades me
to crack the windows open, and she lies,
flat on her belly, body taut, legs stretched out
in her best Superman impression,
her nose picking up the scent of prey
I can't see. Then a man, just outside,
pulls a trigger seven times. We both run;
she to the window and I to hide
in the back of the closet where
I can't hear the calls for help anymore.
I finally come out, flat on my belly,
crawling, to join her at the window
and watch the cops collect spent casings
from my lawn. She bumps her head
against my arm as if to say,
Everything's all right,
and I scratch behind her ears
as if I believe her.

Liver, Unremarkable

And so too, the kidneys, the intestines,
the spleen; even his heart, unremarkable,
intact in its pericardial sac. But they've broken him
down like a chicken, split-breasted,
although they left his legs and wings.
He's a pile of commonplace parts,
like brake pads in the junkyard
where he scavenged the pieces for his first car,
an old red junker his dad said would never go,
drained, or nearly so, of blood and bile
and piss and shit, and all the things
that greased his body. If he could,
he'd make a joke about shriveling
like a raisin, like the dried out end
of the umbilical cord dropped
from his week-old daughter,
whose infant wails morphed
into the screams of grown women
as the bullets tore through his head
and lodged in his neck, where they're harvested
now. The lethal projectile traveled downward,
slightly to the right; they trace its path,
a finger on a map. Finally, something
to remark – manner of death: homicide.

June 1, 2020

He perches on the roof ledge
and watches the protesters move
through the street, their chants clear
despite my closed window.
I watch him, shirtless gargoyle,
armed only with his camera.
When the helicopter comes,
drops low enough to bend the trees,
he shoots, capturing the red cross
painted on its fuselage, and then the havoc
in the street below. Later, someone
will tell me it was a Medic Huey,
the same chopper that rescued my father
after he humped out of the Vietnam jungle,
carrying his friend on his back,
both choking on some chemical deployed in the name
of freedom. The man is gone, the street quiet.
Only a few stragglers remain
and a discarded sign in the intersection
that says *I can't breathe.*

Socially Distant

The sparseness of my days:
picking out the perfect peach
at the farmers' market, wandering
the grocery store to grab weekly staples,
buying a bottle of Coke for the man who sits
outside the pharmacy and opens the door;
now – a knock at my door and quick steps
away; grocery delivery, our only interaction short
messages about how ripe the bananas should be.
I have curled into my couch under the weight
of three blankets. Nothing separates
hour from hour but the motion of the sun
and Netflix asking if I'm still watching.

Exhaustion

When I wring out the washcloth
I feel the movement resonate
in my chest, where I imagine
hope exists, its supply as thin
as the cheap toilet paper
I bought too much of in March
when I found it hidden
with the hairbrushes and combs;
back when empty shelves
were photo-worthy – like the days
leading up to a hurricane, before
the storm spawns a tornado
that picks up your house
and scatters it over two square miles
like a game of 52 Card Pickup.

Mood

I am drinking morning tea
when the handle falls off
my favorite mug, spilling
Earl Grey all over my lap.
How cathartic it must have been
for angry Bruce Banner to become the Hulk –
a free pass to smash things, to leave a trail
of destruction in his path.
I imagine emptying my counter
with one swipe of my arm,
the way our Labrador's tail
cleared the coffee table of all our drinks.
The crash of breaking glass,
splash of almost empty pop cans,
a pile of sodden bills waiting
to be paid. Before I can think,
I raise the mug above my head
and hurl it to the ground.
It bounces twice, spins
like a little girl in a party dress,
then rests on its side, handleless,
but perfectly intact.

Dad in Hot-Car Death Was Sexting
with Other Women

To see it in black and white like that –
the darkest sins of a person, a throwaway
sentence that becomes the litter at the bottom
of a birdcage or the stuffing that keeps
the cups ordered from the potter
in North Carolina from clanking together
and fracturing back into the sand
they were made from. The words smear
onto my fingers, leaving tracks across my forehead
when I wipe the sweat off on moving day,
a shadow of the cross the priest smudged
reminding me to remember my death.
The newsprint is a grey stain, letters bleeding
into one another, unreadable, like a centuries-old
epitaph marking another name
in a long line of graves.

Mapping the Curve

Fingers worry the lines
on the tooled leather cover
of the journal now filled
with details of her father-in-law's
penis, which he pronounces
to rhyme with tennis.
Bladder. Urethra. Ureter.
All the lines connecting
entrance to exit she's never
really considered until now,
when they're not working
as they should. "Penis," he says,
like a short turn from penance,
which she's honed to fine art
of self-flagellation, worrying
the lines of her life, covering
the same trails until they wear
thin, threaten to drop her
deep into the waves below.
The cover provides a clear
route for her fingers,
bumping over each stitch
like the beads of a rosary.
She doesn't even know
what she's praying for, just knows
she's sorry – sorry for the ways
their lives have gone awry,
sorry for the words she said,
or didn't, sorry that she's defiled
the pages of a new journal
with notes on her father-in-law's penis.

The Answer

Morning birdsong flutters through my window,
first robins, then blackbirds and wrens.
They learn their songs from their parents,
passing notes from generation
to generation. Once, I heard they sing
to announce their strength – they made it
through the night. I can't see them
from my window; they perch, hidden,
in some tree or on a building ledge, but I lean
forward, purse my lips, and sing back.

Fragile

A jumble of white noise breaks
the silence of the room where I line
a drawer with tiny socks. White,
grey, green, like twig tips
of the tree just outside birthing
spring – timorous, trembling
hope, tissue paper thin, no thicker
than the breath that carries the wish
of dandelion fluff, or a bubble, waiting
for its end at the hands of a toddler
or a stiff breeze.

Zoom In on the Teddy Bear

In a corner of the living room, the tiny baby
my friends brought home nurses, his world still as small
as pink lips latched onto a nipple, surrounded
by baby gear barely older than he is
and six friends huddled close, weeping,
the doctor's news still echoing around us.

I often dream of impending disaster:
tornado bearing down on children playing
in the driveway on a summer afternoon,
their parents cheerfully chatting on the porch.
I call out a warning, but they don't hear.

The perfect first scene of a made-for-tv movie:
camera pans to smiling faces,
chalked hopscotch, waiting teddy bear. Hints
to warn the watcher it's not going to end well –
that teddy bear will reappear, torn to shreds
or floating face down in a puddle.

Later, the phone rings – false alarm –
a healthy baby. His mother weeps, restoring
her dreams for the boy in her lap.
Sometimes the children are called in for dinner.
Sometimes the teddy bear is tucked in under an arm.
Sometimes the doctor calls again.

Waiting

A single feather floats past
so close I cross my eyes to see
its frail fluff, the whole thing no bigger
than the fingernail I just chewed off
waiting for the doctor to call.

My breath catches the feather and it turns
stem over tip, as when I was a child
and a wave caught just so
and set me spinning, making me so dizzy
I couldn't separate sky from sand,

until I found my feet beneath me
and stood, shaking the water and fear
from my eyes, like a woman
in the shower whose fingers find a pea
just under the skin of her right breast.

The little feather finds a perch
and lands, leaning forward, tense,
like a woman waiting for a doctor,
like a woman waiting for a phone call,
like a woman waiting.

Unfinished Pietà

Michelangelo's last sculpture stands, half-finished,
and wilting tourists waving maps-turned-fans
suggest air conditioning is the room's
attraction: the stone itself isn't much –
Mary has two faces,
as if the sculptor couldn't decide
if she should behold her son, or look away
as he lies heavy in her arms, their legs
tangled, weighted down by the block.

I like to imagine Michelangelo
died unexpectedly, chisel and hammer
fallen from his hand, grief sharpened
by unfinished work. But historians
say he lingered a week with a head cold.
He'd already carved away
too much stone, the *Pietà* destined
to be unfinished, pinned to this purgatory,
surrounded by visitors escaping the heat, only
to face all they have left undone.

Antonym: Despair

Too close to the sun, then the crash –
the wing-wearer's warning: don't fly too high –
danger stalks, a lioness hunting, low
to the ground, patient. I do not
wonder. I do not wish. I do not nurture
hope. Stay safe. Still. As in the back of the closet
in a lock-down drill. My chest tightens
at the sight of my nine-year-old nephew
rooting for the underdog, school-color clad.
He cheers his team, wearing hope like armor
'til the bitter end of a three-point loss, his grief
charted in damp tracks down his face.
Maybe the world has nothing better to do
than snuff out magic the way he huffs out
his birthday candles, each diverted wish
darkening the room more. I want to beg him
to lower his expectations: to make disappointment
an uninvited guest. Instead, we talk about
how they *almost won*, his faith in the unlikely
outcome still intact. He sows hope
in my dried-out heart, and waters it
with his tears.

Sisters in the Morning, After the Fight

Grey-skied winter hangs heavy outside
the kitchen window over the sink where
we pass each other like tightrope walkers,
stiff and careful, every step dangerous
as we go about our morning routines.

Spatula on cast iron and spoons in mugs
are soundtracks to our silent dance, each
of us considering what we could have said
until my elbow catches a juice glass
sending it rolling toward the counter's edge.

She catches it, and hands it back. "Thanks,"
I say, and she, "You're welcome,"
the silence shattered, the glass still whole.

On Having Upstairs Neighbors

My mom tried to teach me to tap dance
in the kitchen, the only step she knew:
the shuffle-ball-change.
She taught me jitterbug instead.

Now, overhead a herd of small feet race
from east to west and back again.
They stop just above me
now, big feet joining the little ones,
their laughter running down the walls.
I wonder if they're dancing,
the mother spinning the children
until they fall in dizzy heaps.

When I turned forty, I bought tap shoes,
and now I put them on and dance some love-child
of the jitterbug and shuffle-ball change,
following the footsteps of the family above,
as if I belong with them.

And Also With You

When the priest tells us to pass the peace, everyone turns
and I am surrounded by asses and backs.
I lift my hand, making sure I haven't disappeared.

My hand is solid, I feel my heart
through the vein in my wrist, mark
the lifeline in my palm.

I was an only child, gifted at fading
into the background while the adults talked.
I slip out, and back in, unnoticed.

After, we stand together and say we believe
in one God, the Father almighty, maker
of heaven and earth, of all things seen and unseen.

Elegy for the Unknown

I met my family in Wisconsin
once, a long time ago –
a graduation or wedding, some kind
of life-changing event.
But *family* seems like too strong a word.

A group of related things, says Webster,
all the descendants of a common ancestor,
and by that definition we're all family
if you just go back far enough, or by dint
of a shared block, or school, or job.

What makes us family doesn't make us kin.
Last week my Aunt Midge – identical twin
of my grandmother – died, and I pulled up
her obituary, surprised to see
"Genevieve." All that shared blood.
I didn't even know her name.

A Toast to a Dead Stranger

Standing before Stonehenge, I wonder
what kind of love it would have to be
to convince me to haul boulders for miles
and heave them into a sedimentary valentine.
Or maybe, it wasn't love that beckoned,
but a burning desire to declare their existence.
To know they wouldn't be discarded like the ashes
in a Bud bottle I found in the back of the green cabinet
in my parents' garage. I held it up to the light,
judging its contents not enough
to even be all of him, and wondered
who cared enough to tape his obituary
to the bottle, but not enough to remember
to carry him away. Now he sits on my desk,
my own little Stonehenge.

Remember Me

On the Alaskan tundra the guide warned us
not to walk single file: the squishy earth
learns the shape of feet pressing into its flesh
and keeps the memory for five hundred years,
like a story passed down from generation
to generation. I want to stand still
until the ground memorizes my footprint.

Scientists suggest memory lives in cells
spread across the body – kidney and spleen
a backup drive for the brain. I picture my skin
sloughing off, reinventing itself every seven years,
sending a flurry of stories into the air
for strangers around me to breathe in,
to reinvent, to make part of themselves.

Even when I am gone, leaving no one
to trade my family stories, I will still be here,
in footprints and dust, in the lungs
of the woman reading her book next to me on the train.

ABOUT THE AUTHOR

Dawn E. Morrow writes poems for people who believe they don't like poetry. Although she has made her home in Iowa City, IA, Durham, NC, Chicago, IL, Washington, DC and Alexandria, VA, she is a Jersey Girl at heart. She holds an MFA in Poetry and this is her first collection.

This book is set in Garamond Premier Pro, which originated in 1988 when type-designer Robert Slimbach visited the Plantin-Moretus Museum in Antwerp, Belgium, to study its collection of Claude Garamond's metal punches and typefaces. During the 1500s Garamond—a Parisian punch-cutter—produced a refined array of book types that combined an unprecedented degree of balance and elegance, for centuries standing as the pinnacle of beauty and practicality in type-founding. They were based on the handwriting of Angelo Vergecio, court librarian of the French king, Francis I. Slimbach has created a new interpretation based on Garamond's designs and on compatible italics cut by Robert Granjon, Garamond's contemporary.

Copies of this book can be ordered
from all bookstores including Amazon.

•

For more information on the work of Dawn E. Morrow
visit www.antrimhousebooks.com/authors.html.